THE ICEBERG EFFECT

The Untold Secret Of Affiliate Marketing Success

Dean Holland

The Iceberg Effect

© 2019 Dean Holland

ISBN 978-1-5272-4548-8

"I recommend you read this book thoroughly right away, more than once even. With Dean Holland, you couldn't be in better hands."

- Russell Brunson

DEDICATION

To my mum, Cindy, who sacrificed so much throughout her life to help me become the man I am today. And to my wife, Robyn, for having the patience to support me throughout the years as I took countless risks to chase my dreams.

ACKNOWLEDGEMENTS

So many people have positively influenced my online career that I would struggle to think of strategies or concepts we use today that have not been taught or shared, in some part, by others.

While throughout this book I have aimed to give credit where credit is due, some people deserve special mention and thanks for their part in my journey.

To my first ever mentor online, Alex Jeffreys. Being a student of yours changed the course of my life forever. I don't think I could ever quite repay you for what you've done for me, and I will forever be grateful.

Russell Brunson, I'd been a fan of yours for many years before joining your mastermind program. At the time I became a student of yours I was, as I now laugh, 'rich and miserable'. Your advice and encouragement helped reshape me as an entrepreneur and give new life to my company to move forward and impact the lives of so many more than I could have alone.

Through their products, programs, books and even free content they published, I'd like to mention some special individuals who have made a difference to me throughout the years. In no particular order: Mike Filsaime, Todd Brown, Tony Robbins, Jason Fladlien, Michael Cheney, Les Brown, Mike Michalowicz, Rich Schefren, Michael Masterson, Sam Ovens and Perry Belcher. There will undoubtedly be so many more, so for those who have provided value, thank you!

Finally, thank you to my team. I can't be the easiest person to be with at times, with all my wacky thoughts and complete blind faith in 100% of my ideas to be successful (HA!). I could never accomplish all we do without every one of you. You inspire me to be a better person, and together we are all making a positive difference.

TABLE OF CONTENTS

FOREWORD
By Russell Brunson

It's perfectly OK to want more. More money, more time, more freedom, and above all, the ability to give more to others. The reality is, however, that before you can help others, you must first help yourself. That is exactly what this book is going to show you how to do.

When Dean first came to me in 2015, he had already accomplished a great deal and helped thousands of others start and grow a profitable business online. But he was striving to be better—a trait I admire.

He joined my Inner Circle Mastermind to better learn how to help more of the right people, to attract customers that truly wanted more in life, and to do so in a moral and ethical way.

During the years since, I've seen him grow as an individual and develop his training and coaching company to become one of the leaders in the industry, helping vast numbers of people achieve higher levels of success.

Affiliate marketing as a business model is a powerful and proven way for anyone to get started using the internet to grow an income, but as with everything in business, marketing and sales processes evolve over time and, as entrepreneurs, we must learn to adapt with them. What Dean lays out in this book is a clear and precise blueprint that every affiliate marketer needs to know to thrive in today's economy in the most sustainable and profitable way.

I recommend you read this book thoroughly right away, more than once even. With Dean Holland, you couldn't be in better hands.

Russell Brunson
Co-Founder of ClickFunnels
www.ClickFunnels.com

INTRODUCTION

It was 2004. I was 20 and working in a pub in Nottinghamshire, England. Yes, the home of Robin Hood and all the tales that have come with it.

A year earlier, I had started a mobile food truck business where I'd stand in my little portable trailer every day, offering fast food and breakfast items.

The food industry had been my passion since I left school at 16 to work as a waiter in a roadside restaurant. The pay had been low but I discovered I had great talent in customer service and thrived in such an environment.

Knowing that gave me the restaurant bug, and I pushed weekly to learn more about the business, continually approaching my boss for promotions into better-paying positions. Within three years, I went from a humble waiter on minimum wage, to training as a chef, and eventually I joined the management team of the restaurant where I was responsible for ordering from wholesalers, end-of-day accounting, managing shift staff, as well as the overall management of the business during my days of work.

But I wanted more. I wanted to be rich!

As a kid, both my parents worked full-time jobs and provided for my every need. Don't get me wrong, we weren't wealthy by any means, but we weren't poor either. As a young kid growing up, I had a fascination with the finer things in life. I'd watch videos and TV shows in which I would see Rolex watches, mansions and Lamborghinis, and I had a huge love for hip hop music, with videos that would portray the artist living the high life, from which I took huge inspiration. I dreamed of having it all.

Then one day a lightbulb went off:

"I can cook. I have wholesale contacts. I can start my own business, be my own boss and get rich beyond my wildest dreams!"

I began to research my options, but I didn't have the funds to open a restaurant. Then my mum gave me the idea of a food truck. Having a lifelong passion for horses, my mum would take me to shows where we'd see catering services offering things like burgers and hotdogs.

That was it! I could get my own food truck and make my fortune doing what I knew how to do best: cooking and serving food to the public.

Doing my research, I discovered I could pick up a second hand food truck with all the equipment I'd need for about three grand, a fraction of what a traditional premises would cost. Young and short on funds, I turned to my number one investor, my mum. To help, as mums do, she came through and lent me the funds to set up this business. Full of ambition and excitement, I was convinced this was my ticket to everything I could ever want, and so began my first real entrepreneurial venture.

After getting approval from the local authorities to operate a food truck, I found a location where I could offer my products to drivers out on the roadside, Monday through Friday.

The business exploded fast. I'd positioned my truck close to a high school, and word spread fast that the students could buy delicious food, which was superior to the offerings in the school café.

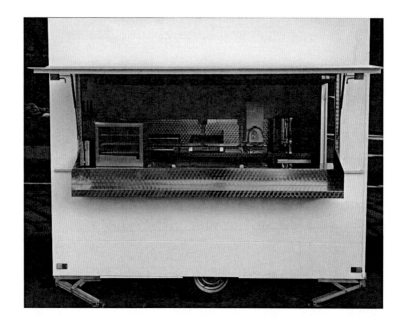

At about 12:15 pm every weekday, I'd be swamped with teenagers buying their lunch, and every day I made hundreds of pounds in revenue. By 2:00 pm my day was done and, working half the time, I made more in a day than I did in a week in my previous job.

I was on top of the world! Just nineteen years old and I was feeling the effects of financial success for the first time in my life. It felt incredible.

My quick success, however, soon had a setback. As it turns out, schools rely in part on food sales from their café at lunch to fund them. But I was taking a lot of their business, which led to them complaining to local authorities who subsequently ordered me to stop serving the kids at lunch time. URGH! A big chunk of daily income was gone overnight.

It sucked.

Still, all was not lost. I had the passing trade of the drivers and commuters, so while it was a big loss, I was still pulling in good income – until a fateful day that ended my food business forever.

Just after a busy lunchtime ended, a car pulled up. Three guys approached and looked at the menu options. There was nothing odd or suspicious about them, and we had the typical small talk. Then one of the guys ordered an unusual number of items, which sent me into a busy panic.

"Hurry, we're in a rush," he said. "I need to get the food to the guys."

He continued to keep me busy, talking about how they were in a rush as I frantically raced back and forth to deliver what he wanted. Within fifteen minutes, I delivered everything and he paid. I put the payment into my tin and the car drove off. Feeling like a job well done and a good chunk of money had been earned, I was content with myself for a moment.

But suddenly something didn't feel quite right; I had this strange feeling in my gut. I opened the door to my food truck and looked down to see the generator that powered the truck had been stolen. Stupidly, it was turned off at the time as we had to do that periodically to prevent it from overheating, and these thieves clearly knew they could take it without my noticing as long as they kept me distracted, which they did. Just like that, I'd lost a key part of what I needed to run my business!

At this point in my life I didn't own a mobile phone and so I was stuck alone, unable to contact anyone. I sat there that day on the edge of the roadside in tears, ashamed that I'd been stupid enough to allow this to happen, shuddering at the thought of what could possibly have happened to me if I'd caught them in the act. The experience shook me up so much that I never took the truck out again. My first business was over, and once again I needed a job.

A friend of my mum was looking for staff at their pub and they gave me a shot even though I had no experience. But the job only paid £1,000 per month, less than I'd ever earned. Just weeks earlier I was earning that much every two days working part time in my food truck.

Although I took the pub job, very quickly I found myself wanting more. Not only was I on low pay but I was also working two shifts a day, six days a week. I'd be working whilst my friends would be meeting up in the pub to socialize. I felt I should be with them and not slaving away for very little return.

More money, more time, more freedom, that's what I wanted to get back and so, one day, I went online and began my search for ways to make some extra money. At this stage I was no longer thinking of making millions, but rather I just wanted to make life a little more comfortable.

Who knew the rabbit hole I would find myself walking down and the years of absolute hell I was about to endure.

Disaster, Debts and Shame

As I searched the Internet for ways to make more money, in no time at all I discovered unlimited options. From posting mail order catalogues, to taking surveys, network marketing, selling on eBay, CD production, affiliate marketing, and even getting paid to become a test subject for trial drugs.

I read as much free information as I could. A get-rich-quick junkie, I'd find articles, websites, blogs and forums. As the weeks went by, I'd subscribe to dozens of email lists to access more free training or downloads.

Soon enough my email inbox was stuffed with offers to buy information products that promised to reveal the closely guarded secrets of the millionaire that had put together the training – from blogging courses, to traffic generation, email marketing and so much more. I was sucked in fast and soon spent money on everything that came my way. And boy it came fast!

I'd log into my email inbox to find five, ten, twenty or more new offers for the latest 'must have' new products. There were software programs that promised to flood my websites with traffic, plugins that claimed to make money in three clicks of the mouse, and countless training courses that weren't even complete once you got into them!

I tried everything, and I do mean everything! Of course, I didn't have the money for all these purchases. So, obsessed, I decided to get credit cards and in no time I had my first MasterCard and Visa and my debts began to pile up. Feeling like my financial situation was getting worse, I didn't tell a soul and made sure to get the mail before anyone else did.

In spite of all my efforts online, nothing worked!

I dabbled in a network marketing opportunity but couldn't get a single signup. I promoted a hosting company in an MLM (multi-level marketing) opportunity by posting flyers in the street. I tried paid advertising through Google to promote a digital training product but lost nearly a grand in twenty-four hours as I had no idea what I was doing.

And then something really appealed to me: affiliate marketing, a type of performance-based marketing in which a business rewards one or more affiliates for each lead or customer brought by the affiliate's own marketing efforts.

The more I learned about it, the more it drew me in. And there was no shortage of online experts, showing off their Ferraris and mansions, happy to share their get-rich wisdom for a price – a price I paid over and over, sinking deeper and deeper into debt as I got more and more out of control.

My life was a mess.

By the time 2008 hit, I had spent four long years trying to make money on the Internet. Rather than riches, I'd found myself with five credit cards, all but one maxed out, and two significant bank loans. I'd blown over £47,000 and failed to make one single sale online, in spite of a head full of information and a computer full of products and software.

Ashamed, I couldn't find the courage to tell anyone about the mess I was in. I was 24 years old and my life was a lie. Having left my job at the pub, I was now working an unskilled job at a construction company. At least I had access to a computer and could go online, although this also added to my growing collection of digital dust on my hard drive.

Years earlier my parents had divorced and I was living with my mum in a small two-bedroom home. For years I'd successfully kept my debts a secret for fear of disappointing her, but it was getting tougher. Debt collection agencies would send mail, creditors would call the landline, and one time, debt collectors even visited the house, though thankfully I was the only one home and didn't answer the door.

Then, one day, my worst nightmare had come true. I walked through the door after a hard day's work to discover my mum had opened a final demand letter for payment from NatWest, one of the banks I had got a credit card from. I owed several thousand pounds on that card and was months behind on payments.

That evening, I had to have one of the toughest conversations of my life. Eyes down, my voice tremoring, I owned up to my mum about what had been going on – at least part of the truth as, out of fear, I didn't share the full extent of my situation. Even so, my mum was disappointed in me.

That was undoubtedly the lowest point of my life. Even today that feeling of shame drives me forward so I never again have to experience the devastation of having to admit I was a complete failure.

In hindsight though, it was a blessing. Hitting rock bottom forced me to evaluate my life and figure out how to turn it around.

That turning point all started with an email.

CHAPTER 1
TURNING MY LIFE AROUND

"Meet Me in London, I'm Paying."

That was the subject line of an email in my inbox. Curious, I clicked open the email. Lucky I did. Seeing those six words on that day would go on to change my life forever.

It was an invitation from a UK marketer from whom I'd bought products and followed for some time. The email said he would be attending an Internet marketing seminar in London and he would pick up a ticket for the first ten people who replied, and meet them at the event.

Convinced that this guy had the key to online success, I felt excited about the prospect of going. But I also felt terrified of coming face-to-face with him as I feared he would learn the truth about what a failure I was.

All day, I thought anxiously of that email.

"Should I reply…?" "Do I ignore it…?"
"If I go, what will people think of me…?"

In my head, I kept hearing the voices of the doubters in my life – family, friends and work colleagues telling me constantly that my desire to have an online business was a dumb pipedream. *"A scam,"* they would say. Give it up and focus on working hard in my job to create a career.

Were they right? Perhaps I can't do this? Should I just give it all up?

And so I struggled with what to do. The next day, though, I built up the courage to reply, believing I would be too late and the ten spots would be filled. The following day, I opened my inbox and couldn't believe my eyes!

"Hey Dean! Good to hear from ya, you're 1 of the 10…………"

Oh. My. Gosh.

Still, I hesitated about going, too fearful he would find out the truth about me. After much deliberation, I knew I had to turn things around. I needed to get out of my comfort zone to face that which scared me. And so I made plans to get to London for those two days.

I arrived in a jacket from my job, four sizes too big for me as I couldn't afford to buy myself clothes. After booking a room at the hotel, I had no money left. I didn't know how I would get food or drink for the next two days, but at least I was there.

As I made my way to the arranged meeting point, I saw Alex Jeffreys (the marketer who'd invited us) and only one other guy. As it turned out, only two of the ten showed up, and the other guy ended up leaving, so it was only me and Alex!

I was in awe of Alex. He was a man I'd followed online for a long time; he was doing exactly what I wanted to do. He was making a fortune as an affiliate marketer, and here I was face-to-face with him in real life. I couldn't believe my luck.

Over the next two full days, we hung out, along with several other full-time marketers. It was like a dream. I was surrounded by Internet marketing gurus I'd followed for years online. Incredibly generous, these guys bought me drinks and paid for meals, not even knowing I was too poor to buy my own.

During those two days I was open and honest about my experiences. Alex gave me advice and direction: be honest and share with the world my honest experiences and struggles. The idea was daunting. All you ever saw online then was people touting their success, and here I was being told to share what a mess I was in. With no options left I knew I had to take his advice, and as tough as the truth would be to admit, I was determined to do everything in my power to make something good happen. When I returned home, I started a blog and began posting the truth about what I'd gone through during my years on the Internet.

Soon after, using the last bit of credit I had available, I joined Alex's coaching program and learned new key skills. I learned how to use my blog effectively, how to get traffic (people) to it, how to build an email list, and finally how to promote affiliate offers for commissions. Soon, hundreds of people shared similar struggles on my blog of trying to make it online. For the first time I felt that I wasn't alone; there were others out there who could understand my pain and frustration.

Five weeks after I attended that seminar I made my first affiliate commission online, finally proving to myself that not only was it possible to make money on the Internet, but I could do it too. I soon learned that once you can make one sale, you can make two, and ten, and one hundred, and one thousand and more.

Nine months later, in July of 2009, I left my construction job to become a full-time Internet marketer and never looked back. Today, through a variety of ventures, I'm responsible for selling over ten million dollars of products online, and I'm blessed to say my life is a far cry from how it used to be back then.

While I learned many marketing tactics from Alex, none of those skills would have made any difference had I not learned far more important lessons, the same ones I shall now share with you.

CHAPTER 2

SUCCESS STARTS WITHIN

Becoming a Winner

When I was eight years old, I attended a sports day at school, with the kids taking part in various races and other challenges whilst the parents stood on the sidelines frantically cheering their child on.

Some of the parents would say to their kid, *"Try your best, son. It's the taking part that counts."* Not my mum. Competitive, she would say things like, *"Get out there and win; second place is the first loser."* The idea that you must do all you can to win always stuck with me, and striving to be the best is how I approach everything I do.

Make no mistake, I play to win. If I believe in something, I will invest in myself, take calculated risks to achieve it, and nothing will stop me.

If I've decided to get in better shape, I'll research for countless hours and buy the equipment and supplements needed. If I'm learning a hobby or sport, I'll watch countless hours of training and tutorials, or get a coach where possible.

And not just because of my mother's words. All the setbacks, failures and tough challenges I have experienced made me the way I am; you have to be relentless in your pursuit of getting what you want in life.

Attitude is everything. Your mindset is what determines actions you take or not, and without any doubt it's the most important factor we all must continually develop to improve upon.

Every morning I wake up and go through a set daily pattern. Part of that routine is to listen to something inspirational, motivational and even educational whilst I take a shower. That's often Les Brown, one of my favourite inspirational people, to put me in an amazing frame of mind, so I can make the most of my day.

One of my favourite quotes of his is: *"Your past or present does not have to define your future."*

Despite all the losses I experienced early on, stuck in dead-end jobs with minimal prospects for future success, I never lost hope, even when I hit rock bottom. Deep inside, I believed it was possible to achieve more, make more, create more, be more.

Whilst everyone is unique, the bad habits or self-limiting beliefs holding people back often fit into one of three categories: mindset, fears or attitude.

Let's start by looking at growth vs. fixed mindset.

Growth vs. Fixed Mindset

Let me share with you a story about two guys, John and Bob, who both joined our *Internet Profits Accelerator* program on the same day.

On the first day, John started progressing through our training and joined our private community group where he was welcomed by our other Partners, or as we call ourselves, "The Internet Profits Family."

"I'm going to be one of your biggest success stories," he said.

Within a few days, he had posted a picture of himself holding his certificate, which showed he had completed our initial training, had passed the quiz and was now certified as one of our Internet

Profits Partners. He told us he was going to spend a couple of hours every evening after he finished working at his day job to follow our guidance to start building his business.

Within his first thirty days of joining, John was up and running, getting traffic, building his email list, and a few weeks later, he was generating an income. It wasn't thousands but he'd made his first few hundred bucks. This was an enormous achievement as he had tried various online ventures over a five-year period, before working with us, with no results at all. Within six months, John was making four figures a month in his business and continues to focus today on growing that.

So, what about Bob? Well, we didn't hear anything from Bob for about two weeks. Then he requested to join the community group. Unlike John, though, Bob didn't post anything or make any comments when we welcomed him. After a month, Bob told us he'd been distracted and couldn't remember how to log into the members area. Of course, we quickly provided him the details and information he needed. Bob didn't respond to our reply, but we could see from our tracking that he had now logged in, so we assumed all was well.

Bob was retired and, according to him, he was putting in up to six hours a day at the computer. This meant he could experience faster progress than someone like John, who put in about two hours each day. But that was not the case, and six weeks after joining, he again asked politely for the login details.

I asked Bob why he kept losing his account details. He said he had been busy since joining as he had also purchased several other courses after he joined ours, and he was doing a little of all of them each week.

I advised Bob that if he continued to try and do everything he would actually hinder his progress and it would likely not get him the results or business he claimed to want. Bob agreed with me, and in his words, he said, *"I'll try to do better."*

That was about seven months ago at the time of writing this and, to date, Bob hasn't progressed much further at all.

Why would this be? Why would two people with access to the same information, the same tools, resources and even support experience completely different outcomes? Why would one hit the ground running whilst the other does nothing?

I venture to guess that Bob had a fixed mindset and was stuck in his ways, while John was not.

Fixed Mindset

According to psychologist Carol Dweck, people with fixed mindsets believe their skills and talents to be based on inherent character, intelligence, and creative ability. This is set in stone and they can't be changed. If you succeed, you attribute your success to the stuff with which you were born.

What do you do? You stay within your comfort zone and avoid failure at all costs by not even trying. As a result, failure defines you.

And so you might not try to market online because you fear you will never get a sale. Stuck in a fixed mindset, you don't make any effort to push past this fear.

Growth Mindset

People like John have a growth mindset. They believe that they can be good at what they try because their abilities and skills depend not just on inherent nature but on actions.

Thriving on challenge, people like John, and myself, view failure as a temporary setback and springboard for growth. This gives us confidence to push into unfamiliar territory where we are always growing and learning something new.

In her book *Mindset: the New Science of Success*, Carol Dweck explains how Michael Jordan, by having a growth mindset, became Michael Jordan.

Believe it or not, Jordan was cut from his high school basketball team. Did he give up? No. He took this as a sign that he needed to work harder than anybody else in the world. And that's what he did.

In six short years, he graced the cover of Sports Illustrated with the caption '*A Star is Born*' and became the best basketball player the world has ever seen.

And he did this, explains Dweck, by believing that through hard work and dedication, he could improve enough to get to the NBA – a growth mindset!

This isn't always easy. Society and, often, our families, program us to conform to their values and to answer to someone else's agenda. The result is that we go on a journey of living their truth, not our own.

Refuse to do so. Follow your own heart and passion, not someone else's. And, importantly, believe in yourself.

If I gave into self-doubt, you wouldn't be reading this book now. It was only because I was furious at myself for being such a loser that I managed to crawl up and eventually break through. I'll tell you one thing: on my death bed, I'd rather regret the things I did in my life, than regret the things I did not do.

What about you?

Fears

Most of us have fears that stop us from taking the steps needed to get what we want out of life. I'm not talking about the fear of snakes, fire, violence or strangers. Humans are driven for survival; these fears are a necessary mechanism to keep us alert for danger.

I'm talking about the fears inside your head, like being too afraid to speak up lest you be judged poorly by others. Remember how terrified I was to even go to that Internet marketing conference because I feared Alex would find out what a loser I was?

Why did I end up going? I realized I had to face my fears if I ever wanted to meet my dreams. Don't let your fears stop you from your dreams. Instead, face and befriend them now.

Fear of Failure

Do you avoid doing things to avoid failure? Of course you do. Everyone does.

But many people push past this fear to succeed. And that's what you must do. If not, your fear of failure will rule your actions and decisions, and you will never take the necessary steps to become the captain of your ship. Even worse, fear of failure could prevent you from even trying something new.

The question is, then, how can you overcome your fear of failure?

Firstly, be willing to take risks to go after what you want, knowing you will experience setbacks, and at times you won't get the result you hoped for, and that's OK. Contrary to what we tell ourselves, failure is not always a bad thing; to me it means progress. I've learned far more from the times things didn't work out than when they did! I implore you to change your mindset to seeing failure as a stepping stone and not an end in itself. When you fail, reassess the situation and ask yourself what you could have done differently, or better, to achieve a different outcome. Take note of how or why it happened so you can avoid the same path in future.

Use Thomas Edison for inspiration: *"I have not failed. I've just found 10,000 ways that didn't work."*

Also, stop imagining the worst-case scenario.

If you are in the habit of ruminating over all that could possibly go worse, change the way you think now. I see so many times people focus on the worst-possible outcome, and say things like, *"What if I do this and I fail?"*

You know what I say? *"What if I do this and I succeed!"* When you stop viewing failure as an end and instead understand it means you're making progress, you can stop fearing failure and embrace the fact there are going to be times when the outcome you get is not that which you desired, but with each failure you are one step closer to success.

Fear of Success

Not only may you resist change because of a fear of failure, but you may also resist change because of a fear of success. It sounds crazy, but it's a real stumbling block for many, and not everyone is consciously aware it's affecting them.

Why would this be? Well, think about it. Having more freedom, more money and more recognition can create changes in your life, and as we know, change can be scary. There are gains but there are also potential restrictions, responsibilities and alterations to your life.

For instance, you might believe that success may mean having less time to relax, do exercise, or even be with your family and friends. Perhaps, in your mind, making more money, while great, could also mean you will make more money than your partner does, and this could cause a rift in your marriage.

And then there are all those people who will be coming to you for loans. If you say, *"Sorry, Buddy,"* it could cause friction in your relationships. Making more money also likely means more responsibilities and hours worked.

To become a success, you must get past the fear of success. Sure, it may well bring about changes in your life and potentially cause some problems. But those problems are a lot more manageable than failing in life and not living out your dreams.

We will always have problems, but the problems you face when you're broke are far worse than those faced with money and freedom. Making more money gives you options, and with more options you have the ability to bring about positive change in the world for you and for others, so don't allow anything to stop you from making a difference.

Attitude

I had the good fortune of meeting Tony Robbins once backstage after my wife and I had gone through a six-hour seminar with him. More than most, Tony has helped me with attitude and mindset. I'll never forget the lessons he shared about controlling your emotional state.

During this talk, he would explain that we can choose how we feel in any given moment, whether it be stressed, angry, happy, sad or regretful.

At first, my reaction was to disagree. I thought of numerous instances that had stressed or angered me, such as a former boss treating me badly. I firmly believed that in these moments it was always someone else that caused me to feel the stress or anger, not myself. They were the ones treating me poorly, and they were the ones making me stressed!

But as I continued to listen to Tony, soon enough I began to see things differently. He explained that no matter what situations occur in life, we get to choose how we feel and how we deal with the matter.

If someone mistreats you, the natural tendency is for you to feel bad, and it's likely been this way your entire life. That means it's not a quick fix to change the way you deal with things; taking conscious control of your emotional state isn't a natural process for most, but if you actively work on it you can make it so.

Here's the key: when you feel a strong emotion, like sadness or anger, learn not to react instantly, but take a moment and step back. This gives you time to think before you react, and to take control of your emotions so negativity doesn't drag you down.

I worked to overcome reacting immediately by understanding that feeling anger, frustration, disappointment, sadness, regret and so on, would not make the situation any better but only worse. So why would I choose to put myself in that state?

In your journey to start an online business you've likely experienced many setbacks, as I did; you cannot allow these negative experiences to impact your future decisions.

Think Positive Thoughts

Your attitude and the mindset you adopt significantly impact the outcome and results you achieve. No amount of marketing tactics or strategies can help us if we first do not work on ourselves.

Consider this question: How confident are you that you can succeed? If the answer is, *'not sure'* or *'not very'* then you won't. You must believe in yourself or you won't take all the necessary steps to become a success.

The only way to remove uncertainty is to change your thinking from *'it won't work'* to *'I will make it happen'*. From *'I'm not smart enough to succeed'* to *'I have all the capabilities I need to succeed'*.

In other words, you need to think positively. And to do this you must rewire your brain out of the negative *'I can't do it'* mode to the positive *'I can do anything I want'* mode.

Every time you think a negative thought, you strengthen the worry cycle in your brain. This keeps you obsessing, dragging, losing sleep, feeling miserable and making others around you miserable.

The negative frame of mind pushes away the people around you, and the resources you need to get what you want. As a result, you keep sabotaging your chances at success.

Stop self-sabotaging now. Think positive. Say things like *'I am a winner!', 'I can do it!'* and *'I am the master of my fate!'* When you do, your brain releases feel-good hormones. Over time, those areas of the brain that stimulate positive feelings strengthen, and this changes the entire biochemistry and the structure and function of your brain. Slowly, negative thinking diminishes, replaced by more rational, balanced thinking.

Stop Playing Victim

Start now to banish self-limiting beliefs. When you are negative, you are surrounded by a wall of self-limiting beliefs. With this mindset, you feel like a victim of your circumstances and blame something or someone else for your problems. For instance, *"It's not my fault that I didn't get it done. My boss gave me too much work so I didn't have time."*

This victim mindset comes from feeling that outside forces control you. *"She makes me nervous,"* or, *"He made me do it."* This also means that you give power over to someone or something outside yourself to control how you feel or what happens to you. The result is you do nothing because you feel too powerless to change anything.

Take Responsibility

In my first four years trying to make money on the Internet, I was sceptical of, and resented, others. I'd say things like, *"The gurus are lying to me; they don't want me to succeed."* Then it occurred to me: though I was sold many bad products, *I was the one buying them. I* was the one making the bad decisions, over and over without taking personal responsibility for the outcome. Only when I accepted that did I allow myself to move forwards positively.

To achieve success, you must feel in charge and in control of what happens to you. You alone must take responsibility for what happens to you and stop blaming others, or you will continue to make poor choices just as I did. Instead, embrace the philosophy that you make things happen in life, rather than believing that life is happening to you.

Believe that you are the captain of your ship, the master of your fate, and that everything, including achievements, relationships, health and physical fitness, is in your control. In other words, you must take responsibility for your actions.

Blaming only attracts more drama and negativity – things you do not want in your life. Instead, take full responsibility for your current condition, and understand that you can change in an instant once you make the decision to do so.

CHAPTER 3

FINDING YOUR WHY

If you'd asked me in 2004 why I wanted an Internet business I'd have told you I wanted to make enough money so that I could have more fun in life, go out with friends more often, and one day work for myself again. In other words, my primary motivation was money. For years I stayed stuck and failed to make any money at all.

Why would this be?

To become a success and have your dreams in life come true, you must know not only *what* you want to achieve but, more importantly, *why*. Despite what all the push-button, shiny-object sellers will tell you, starting and growing a business profitably isn't always easy. In fact, it can be highly challenging and tough at times.

It's in these tough times that it becomes even more important to have a deep and clear understanding on why you want more in life. When the challenges arise, you will be more determined to push forward and overcome them because you will have the drive to break through; money alone is never enough.

When I realized this, everything changed. Now, after more than a decade of hard work, many of my goals and dreams are a reality. My businesses make more in one day than I used to make in one month in previous jobs. I have travelled to many countries, seen breathtaking sights and had life-changing experiences. I drive nice cars, live in an amazing five-bedroom home in the English countryside, and I have married the most amazing woman.

I wake up every morning with passion and love for my business, driven by my mission in life: to help others create their dream life using the power of an Internet-based business. It doesn't get better than that.

Discovering Your Why

Once you discover your why, you too can unlock your ability to become a success and fulfil your dreams. To get there, you must know the core reason (or reasons) for wanting to take this path.

Finding this path is like peeling back each layer of an onion.

To help you get to the core of the onion, I've designed a simple exercise: ask yourself *'why?'* until there is no longer an answer to give.

The answers given are mine to show you how to use the process. At the end of this chapter, I have provided you with blank pages to complete this exercise with your own answers.

Let's start.

Question:

"Why do you want an Internet business?"

Answer:

"Because I hate my job."

Why?

"Because I don't make enough money to live how I want to live."

Why?

"Because I want to be able to afford to go out with friends more often, have more fun and become my own boss."

Why?

"Because I want more from my life and don't want to be stuck in this dead-end job forever and never know what success feels like."

Why?

"Because if I don't do better for myself, I'll be viewed as a deadbeat and failure."

Why?

"Because I want to make my wife and mum proud."

Why?

"Because I want to provide my wife with the best life ever, and I hope to

have a family together one day, for which I can fully provide. And I want to provide for my mum. She sacrificed so much for me and I want to be able to give her everything she deserves and for her to know that, against all odds, she did a great job raising me."

Why?

"Because I don't want to be a failure and lose everyone that I love."

Notice how I went from stating I wanted that outcome because I hated my job, to the core reason of not wanting everyone to think I'm a failure and lose everyone I love.

Once I discovered that, my vision became crystal clear. I knew my real '*why*' and could now keep this clear in my mind at every moment, so when I face tough times, I have that drive to propel me forwards.

You must do the same. Knowing your true and real core reason 'why' will motivate you more than ever before to achieve success. Once you discover your purpose for being, you feel never-ending passion and adventure. Instead of dragging yourself out of bed in the morning, you hop out, eager to start your day.

You will sacrifice short-term pleasure for long-term gain. For instance, even though you've had a long day at work, you will feel charged to go home and fire up the computer to get your business going rather than getting together with friends at the nearest pub or binge watching a show on Netflix.

No longer a follower, you will become a leader of your life and of your chosen path, displaying courage, discipline, endurance and self-control.

You will take risks and inspire others to have the same courage.

Fired up, there's no stopping you.

So, start today peeling each layer of the onion and become the unstoppable force you need to be!

"Why do you want an
internet business?"

Why?_____

_____

_____

_____

_____

_____

Why?_____

_____

_____

_____

_____

_____

_____

Why?_____

_____

_____

_____

_____

_____

Why?_____

_____

_____

_____

_____

_____

Why?_____

_____

_____

_____

_____

_____

_____

Why?_____

_____

_____

_____

_____

_____

Why?_____

_____

_____

_____

_____

_____

Why?_____

_____

_____

_____

_____

_____

_____

CHAPTER 4

LIFE BY DESIGN

In my early days in business, I made a huge mistake that cost me: I failed to take the time to figure out exactly what I needed out of my business to be able to live my dream life.

Most people just pluck a figure out of thin air and say something like, *"I need to make at least $10,000 a month online."* Ten grand tends to be the magic number often picked out of one's head willy-nilly.

From this moment onward, vow to make very clear what you want. This will give you direction in what steps to take to pursue your goal.

Having completing the exercise in the previous chapter, you will now be clear on your '*why*'. Now it's time to get clarity on what the dream life looks like, and what is required to make it happen.

The objective of this exercise is to calculate how much per month your business needs to generate for you to live the life of your dreams. By formulating a personalized plan to achieve everything you could ever wish for, you're better equipped to understand your progress and stay on track toward your goal.

In answering the questions, you will see a real and tangible target to work toward. This, combined with your core reason(s) for wanting a profitable business will lay the foundation to making it a reality.

Start now by answering the following questions. This will give you a concrete guide for meeting your goals. I have provided some fill-in-the-blank worksheets at the end of this chapter to help you. If you have a spouse or significant other, I recommend you do this part together. Let yourself go and have fun designing your dream life.

Location

In your dream life, where do you want to live?

In the same country or state you're living now? Or somewhere else?

In a city location? In the countryside or some other location?

One location? More than one?

Find a picture(s) and print them out so you can visually see the dream.

Home

Now that you know where you'd live, in what type of home (or homes) do you want to live?

A conservative three-bedroom place? A luxurious modern mansion with beautiful gardens? A castle? A city apartment? Or something else?

Buy or rent?

Look at the relevant options online. Shop for the home as if you're ready to move now. Find that dream place in which you'd love to see yourself living.

Take note on the purchase or rental price, and if you'd like, print off any pictures so you can visualize that dream home.

Utility Bills

Next, with your best estimation, try to calculate what the utility bills might be on your dream home. Gas, electric, water, insurance policies, and everything else you pay as a homeowner.

If you live in a 1,000-square-foot place and know what your monthly bills are, and your dream home is 6,000 square feet, just multiply your current costs by six.

Vehicles

Would you have any?

If so, how many, and what would they be?

Would you buy brand new, or choose second-hand?

Find those dream vehicles online, print off any pictures and look at how much it would cost to buy your chosen one(s). Take note on the costs and make your best guess at what the monthly payments may be. Some websites will give you this figure, which makes it even easier.

Search online for a rough insurance rate.

Food

What are your monthly food costs? Perhaps you'd eat finer foods than you currently do, or maybe you'd have a chef come in and prepare your meals.

Remember, this is your DREAM life; don't put yourself in a box with restrictions.

Vacations

How many would you take each year?

Where would you go and for how long each time?

How would you fly? Coach? Business? First class?

When you've calculated the cost of your vacations and you've multiplied it by how many you'd have each year, take that figure and divide it by twelve to give you a monthly cost for vacations and write it down.

Recreation/Entertainment

How about any fun times, things like going on dates, buying gifts or toys for loved ones, days out, clothing, pamper days, that type of stuff?

There are lots more you could include as you do this exercise. School, savings, investments, donations or giving of any kind. This is your life, have fun with it.

Keep going until your dream life is designed and you find yourself with a monthly number that you need to earn to live it. Then add appropriate taxes.

For me, I'd add on 30% of the total monthly figure. So, if my figure was $10,000 for example, I'd add on $3,000 for taxes to give myself a total of $13,000 that my business needs to provide me on a monthly basis to live my dream life.

Once you've completed this exercise on the worksheets, it's time to bring some clarity to the specific actions required of you to build your online business.

Life By Design

Location?_____

_____

_____

_____

_____

_____

Total:_____

Home?_____

_____

_____

_____

_____

_____

Total:_____

Utility Bills? _____

_____

_____

_____

_____

_____

Total:_____

Vehicles? _____

_____

_____

_____

_____

_____

Total:_____

Food? _____

_____

_____

_____

_____

              Total:_____

Vacations? _____

_____

_____

_____

_____

              Total:_____

Recreation/Entertainment?_____

_____

_____

_____

_____

Total:_____

Other?_____

_____

_____

_____

_____

_____

_____

_____

_____

_____

_____

_____

Total:_____

Subtotal: _____

Tax: _____

Total Income Goal: _____

CHAPTER 5
THE FOUR CORE
AREAS OF FOCUS

Lost, confused, frustrated, angry. These are just some of the feelings I experienced for years trying to successfully break into affiliate marketing. It seemed like there was always so much to learn and so much to do, all whilst juggling a full-time job and the other commitments in my life.

When added to the fact that every day I'd get new offers for courses that would pull me in totally different directions, with even more new skills to learn, and often with completely contrasting advice, there's no wonder I felt this way!

Truth be told, even when I left my day job to do affiliate marketing full time, those feelings didn't end. I would still often find myself feeling confused again, and I'd be lying if I said even to this day it's not an area with which I battle.

Knowing this was, and continues to be, an area I struggle with, I had to dedicate myself to figuring out exactly what I needed to focus on in order to produce results. To my surprise, the more I simplified my efforts and reduced the number of things I focused on doing, the better my results became. On top of that, the less confusion and frustration I felt!

For years, I had assumed that the more I did, the more likely I was to succeed, but as I have found, that couldn't be further from the truth. I had a huge helping hand in this area when I read *80/20 Sales and Marketing* by Perry Marshall, which details how to apply what is known as the Pareto principle to your business.

In simple terms, the Pareto principle states that 80% of your results will come from 20% of your efforts. Therefore, if you can figure out what those 20% of efforts are, you can focus most of your time on them to see a positive improvement in results.

With this understanding, I began to do an hour-by-hour study of my activities each day by simply writing down on a piece of paper what I was doing every hour during my time at the computer.

The results of the exercise were shocking! What became clear to me first and foremost was the staggering amount of time each day I was wasting on general stuff that would never contribute towards income. Checking emails, trawling social media, checking Skype, answering phone calls from friends and taking trips to the store; these are just some of the things that would show up on my time-tracking sheet every day.

Looking at them individually right now you might think, as I once did, that these things aren't that bad and probably need to be done. But what if I were to tell you that checking emails would be thirty minutes a day, social media would be one hour a day, and checking Skype another twenty minutes? Just those three activities alone would be nearly two hours each day. Now, multiply that by twenty working days in a month and you've got a staggering forty hours per month spent on non-income producing activities. That's a typical working week every single month wasted! Worryingly, most people never take the time to even consider where their time is going and yet time is the only thing we can never get back, so it's critical that it's invested wisely.

You'd be well advised to put yourself through a similar exercise for the next seven days. If you're spending two hours a day working on your business, write down everything that you do during that time on a daily basis. You must do so with complete and total honesty. There's no point tricking yourself.

Find out how your time is spent and then you can ensure that it's not going to waste. It's critical that you focus your time on activities that contribute towards income, as anything else is simply going to delay you reaching your goals.

The question is, then, what are the income-producing activities that you should focus your time on? Here's the good news: there are only four of them, and when you make these core areas the focal point of your time and efforts, you will be able to experience positive progress in your business.

CORE FOCUS #1: TRAFFIC

For many years, the art of traffic generation to me meant aimlessly throwing my affiliate links anywhere and everywhere I could in desperate hope that maybe someone would click them and buy, which of course they didn't.

As I would discover, nothing happens if there's no traffic being generated in your business. It doesn't matter how great your websites look or how incredible the offers you're promoting are, because if you cannot get enough of the right people to see them, you'll get no results.

The first thing you should understand about traffic is you will ALWAYS pay for it in one form or another. Whilst you'll undoubtedly hear claims of 'free traffic' everywhere you turn online, I want you to know that there's no such thing. Every visitor you generate has been paid for in either time (organic traffic) or money (paid traffic), or a combination of the two.

In the early years of my business, I had more time than money and so that is what I invested to start getting traffic to my affiliate links. It was a slow and laborious process, but it's what I had to work with at the time. Eventually, I would be able to start investing a percentage of my income into paid advertising and was able to get traffic much faster than any organic efforts had previously done.

It was learning from Russell Brunson that would give me a better understanding of the three types of traffic we have at our disposal:

1. **Traffic you control**
2. **Traffic you don't control**
3. **Traffic you own**

The big goal is to own your traffic, meaning to be able to send it where you want, when you want, without having to pay more for it. Before we get further into that, let's first look at the other two types of traffic.

Traffic You Control

To control traffic means you are able to direct it to where you want it to go. Any form of paid advertising gives you the ability to direct traffic to a website or link of your choosing. You do not own this type of traffic, the platforms you are advertising on do. You can, however, pay them some money to take control of the flow of some of their visitors.

Some examples would include the following:

- **Pay-per-click advertising**
- **Banner advertising**

- **Native advertising**
- **Email advertising**

Mastering the skill of paid advertising is one I recommend you commit to. In my experience most people, just as I was, are terrible at it initially and lose money, but in time, as you further develop your skills, you will get better and, in no time at all, you can become great.

Traffic You Don't Control

This type of traffic is a result of organic efforts made by you or others. There's no way to predict how much of this traffic will show up or when it may do so. There are many factors that can impact the results of organic traffic, some of which are completely out of your control.

Some examples would include the following:

- **Blogging**
- **Search engine optimization**
- **Social media**

- **Forums**
- **Video sharing sites**
- **Press releases**

I believe organic content creation and publishing has a serious place in business online and should be strongly considered. The results from it may not be under your control, but one thing is for certain: the more quality content you put out into your marketplace, the more people can find you, get to like you and gain trust in you, the compounding impact of which can grow very strong over time by your being consistent with it.

Traffic You Own

This is the holy grail of traffic and is what all other forms of traffic should be guided towards – taking ownership of it. To own the traffic means you have already paid the cost of it and no longer have to do so. You can communicate with this traffic, give advice to this traffic, share value with this traffic, and make offers to this traffic, all without having to lay out further payment to direct it anywhere you so choose.

Today, we live in the most amazing times where we can own traffic in multiple different ways, at least in part, by building audiences on popular platforms online. This can include social media fans/followers, YouTube channel subscribers, and a whole host of other such audiences that you can build, and whenever you so choose, direct to anywhere you wish.

That said, I would never say you FULLY own the traffic in these instances, because let's be honest, platforms come and go, and if they go, your audiences are gone with them.

For that reason, the only true and real way you can own your traffic is when you own the contact information of the people in your audience and have permission to communicate with them using it.

Therefore, you absolutely must capture your traffic and audience onto an email list as we shall now discuss.

CORE FOCUS #2: CAPTURE

The second focus is all about building a database of contacts from the traffic that you generate. As an affiliate marketer, this typically means to build your own email list of people that you can communicate with whenever you so choose. That's not to say you cannot collect other information, such as name, phone number or address, but commonly speaking it's typical to capture a person's email address so you can communicate with them via that channel.

Looking back over my career, if I could do anything differently, I would have definitely started to build an email list much sooner than I did. I'd heard countless times, for years, of people building email lists and making vast sums of money, but I had always feared that no one would actually listen to me. And if they did, what if I said the wrong thing or they didn't like me? These concerns caused me not to bother moving ahead with it for years, which was a mistake.

When I did start to build an email list and communicate regularly with the people on it, to my surprise people were opening my emails and clicking my links. Initially, I'd email them about my latest blog posts and send them there to read them, which they did. Soon enough, I began to recommend certain products as an affiliate that I knew would benefit them, and a percentage of my subscribers would buy based upon my recommendation. It didn't take long for me to learn that your email list can become the most valuable asset you own in your business.

To build your email list, you're going to need three things:

- **Autoresponder**
- **Something of value to offer for free (AKA – the bribe)**
- **Capture pages**

Autoresponder

An autoresponder is the software that stores your contacts' information, such as their email address. Once someone opts in to your email list within your autoresponder and gives you permission to communicate with them, you can then use your autoresponder to send emails to the person's provided email address.

Using your autoresponder, you can send emails in two different ways. The first is to set up and schedule automated follow-up emails to be sent to each contact that joins your list at predefined intervals, such as day one, day three, day five and so on. The other way to send emails is to access your autoresponder at any time you wish and send emails on demand. I'd typically refer to these as broadcast emails, and they would commonly be used whenever you have something new you'd like to share with the people on your list.

An autoresponder is an essential tool in any affiliate marketer's arsenal and something in which you must invest.

Bribe

Your target audience will not just hand over their valuable email addresses to you without good reason to do so. Therefore, you need to make them an offer of something highly desirable that causes them to want to exchange their email address with you in order to receive it.

Typically, this will be some form of digital content that is of value to your target audience. It could be video training, a downloadable PDF, a case study, webinar or useful resource.

The most important factor is not necessarily the form in which the content is created, but more so ensuring that what you're offering is attractive to the exact type of people you want on your email list so that your audience is made up of highly targeted contacts that would benefit from the offers you will be making them.

To give an example, let's consider this book as a product I wish to offer to people to purchase. Whilst this book will be of value to all kinds of entrepreneurs for different reasons, the primary audience is affiliate marketers.

I would therefore want to build an email list of contacts that are actively interested in the topic of affiliate marketing, and so any bribe that I may offer must be highly appealing to that exact group of people.

I could, for example, offer free video training on 'the 5 little-known steps to create a full-time income as an affiliate marketer from scratch'. Or a PDF report on 'how to make affiliate sales using a secret social media method that takes just 10 minutes per day'. For those that requested such free training from me in exchange for their email address, I would have a great degree of certainty that they would not only benefit from ordering a copy of this book, but they would be very interested in doing so should I present the offer to them.

That is the key of your bribe: to ensure that it is building you an email list of contacts that are highly targeted to the solutions you are choosing to offer as an affiliate, in order to earn commissions on sales made.

Capture Pages

In order to build your email list, you need specific webpages that you can direct your traffic to in order to have them presented with your free bribe offer. There are two webpages that you'll need that make up the email list building process:

1. Opt-in page
2. Bridge page

Opt-In Page: The opt-in page is the initial page that you will send your traffic to, also commonly referred to as a 'squeeze page'. This type of page has only one goal: to capture the visitor's email address in exchange for access to the free bribe that you're offering them.

It's typically a very simple page with no distractions. There's an offer for the free bribe you are presenting that leaves the visitor with just two choices: opt in or leave the page. By opting in, they are subscribed to your email list and captured inside your autoresponder ready for follow-up.

Bridge Page: The bridge page is the webpage you immediately direct all your new subscribers to after they enter their email address on your opt-in page. Its purpose is to thank the subscriber for requesting your bribe, inform them how to access it, tell them what they can expect from you, and direct them on what you'd like for them to do next, which would typically be to click a button or link on the page in order to take a look at a product that you are recommending as an affiliate. What exactly you offer here is very important, as you will soon learn later in this book.

CORE FOCUS #3: FOLLOW UP

When you're building an email list, it's important to know that most people will not buy an offer you present the first time they see it, so it's critically important that you have a follow-up process in place.

Having captured your subscriber's contact information within your autoresponder, you can follow up with them via email. The follow-up is not a one-time deal; it's an ongoing process in which you must remain consistent. Never forget, every one of those subscribers you see on your email list is a real person, like you or me, and they have joined your list because they are interested in the topic you presented and have problems they want to solve.

Whilst your goal in following up with your subscribers is ultimately to make sales, it's not the only thing you should be thinking about. Most of the people that join your email list have no idea who you are, what you're about, or even if you can help them. Therefore, it's important that you constantly focus on delivering value in order to get these people to know you, like you and, over time, trust you. Of course, not everyone will, and they can unsubscribe from your list, which is fine and to be expected, but for everyone else you must remain consistent in your follow-up communication to continually nurture that relationship.

I cannot stress enough, this is where the money is made – in the follow-up! The day you stop communicating with your list is the day they begin to forget who you are and, naturally, the day you stop generating any income from your email list asset.

So what do you say and how do you say it? Well, as with everything else, chances are you're not going to be any good when you first start writing emails, and as I keep saying, that's OK! The sooner you start and the more you practise, the better you'll get.

Whenever I'm building an email list, I like to put in place an automated email follow-up series within my autoresponder that spans at least seven days. That way I know that every new subscriber joining my list will hear from me each day during that initial seven-day period. You may or may not wish to email daily but that is my personal preference due to the fact I know people have a lot of other stuff being shown to them every minute of every day, and I want to do my best not to let them forget about me.

During this initial seven day follow-up, I'm aiming to accomplish multiple objectives that include delivering on my promises, establishing a relationship with the subscriber and leading them to the next action I wish them to take, which is typically to make a purchase.

You'll notice that in each email during this follow-up sequence, I include what I'm calling a 'curious cliffhanger'. This stems from a concept I learned from André Chaperon in his *Autoresponder Madness* program, in which he talks about using the same approach in emails as TV soap operas use. If you can think back to a show you've seen on TV, you'll recall that in the last thirty seconds or so, there's always some big thing that happens that they do not fully reveal. The goal is to leave you on the edge of your seat desperately wanting to know what happens next. That is what this curious cliffhanger is all about, teasing the reader and leaving them with a strong desire to receive and open your next email!

Here's a quick breakdown of what that looks like:

Day One: Thank them, introduce yourself, set expectation, deliver on the promise of the bribe, and ask a question that elicits a reply. Then, set a curious cliffhanger for the next email. (As a side note, for those who do reply to you, be sure to respond back.)

Day Two: Share a relevant back story based on personal experience with which the subscriber can likely resonate. This could be a story of struggle, pain or desire. For example, something you have gone through in your pursuit of the desired outcome. Make a light mention of the product you're promoting with a link for them to check it out. The product is positioned here as something that helped you overcome that struggle/pain. Set a curious cliffhanger for the next email.

Day Three: Share a big discovery story. What has been a breakthrough that you've made that has helped you? Tie the story back to the product you're promoting and explain why or how this product helped you personally have that breakthrough. Give the link for them to check out the product with your recommendation that they grab it for themselves. Set a curious cliffhanger for the next email.

Day Four: Detail the big benefits of the product you're promoting. Explain clearly how this product solves a problem they are facing right now. Give a call to action to grab this product now via your link. Set a curious cliffhanger for the next email.

Day Five: Share customer success stories. Ideally, this would be your own success from using the product but it could also be other customers' stories. You're looking to further prove that the product you're offering works and instil more trust in your subscriber to make the decision to order the product. Give your link for them to do so. Set a curious cliffhanger for the next email.

Day Six: Overcome common objections. What questions might the subscriber have that are preventing them from taking action? Use this email to answer them and squash anything that is potentially holding them back with your link to order after you have done so. Set a curious cliffhanger for the next email.

Day Seven: Genuine scarcity and additional incentive. Find a real reason why they must act NOW and where possible add an additional incentive for them to do so on this day. You could include a bonus of some kind as a free gift for them buying today. I'd advise making it only available if they do so on this day. Also, inform them this is the final day you will mention this product and your bonus, and make it very clear they must act right now or they will miss out. Set a curious cliffhanger for the next email.

As you can see, a lot has been accomplished in the first seven days of them joining your email list. You've communicated consistently, delivered on your initial promise of the free bribe they requested and begun to develop a relationship with them, all whilst making sales of the first product you are promoting to them.

Remember, this follow-up communication must not end. Keep the conversations going, keep the value flowing and never, ever stop emailing your list with a healthy combination of information of value and offers that can help them.

Speaking of offers, let's discuss that now.

CORE FOCUS #4: SALES SYSTEM

The fourth core focus is to be making offers to your audience. There's no point driving traffic, capturing people onto your list or following up if you're never going to make offers. That's how money is made!

You must be selective in the products and services you choose to recommend to your audience. Every single recommendation must absolutely have their best interests at heart and not be promoted solely for the purpose of making a quick buck.

I'll be honest with you; when I first began to experience the thrill and income of making money by sending simple emails to my list, I messed up in this area. For a brief period, due to my own lack of experience at the time, I allowed myself to get swept away in the excitement of how easy the money would come in. The bigger my list grew, the more money I'd make by emailing them, and as a young, dumb twenty-something entrepreneur, I found myself caring more about how many sales a promotion would make me rather than how much the product would benefit my subscribers.

It's not something I'm proud of, but it is the truth, and I've seen it happen with countless others too. If you continue to take action and build your list as you should, be aware of how easy it is to fall into this trap and avoid it at all costs. You, too, will feel a buzz hitting send on an email and minutes later seeing money show up in your account – it's immensely exciting. But I can tell you from my mistakes that if what you're recommending is not in your subscribers' best interests, you may make short-term income, but you will jeopardize long-term gains by destroying the relationship you have with those people. It's just not worth it. Treat people right and they will listen to you for many years.

However, there is a problem. As you well know, business is not simply about making sales, but rather it's about making sales profitably. For that reason, WHAT you choose to promote bears more significance than ever before.

Several years ago, I noticed a big shift happening in the affiliate marketing industry. More aspiring affiliate marketers than ever before were failing, and only a select few were making the big money. I predicted the end of traditional affiliate marketing at that time and prepared for it. Sadly for most, my predictions came true. Luckily for you, there is a solution, which you will soon learn.

CHAPTER 6

THE DEATH OF TRADITIONAL AFFILIATE MARKETING

As you are aware, affiliate marketing is about promoting other businesses' products and services in order to receive compensation (commissions) for the sales you generate. By all accounts, it's the easiest way to start an online business as you need to learn the fewest new skills compared to other options.

There's no product creation, no building of complex sales processes, credit card processing or customer support that you have to deal with. These are just some of the reasons affiliate marketing appeals to most starting out in Internet marketing.

Still, numbers don't lie, and it's no secret that an overwhelming majority of those who get into affiliate marketing fail to get any significant results. Worse still, just as I did in my early years, most aspiring affiliate marketers experience significant financial losses and end up feeling lost, frustrated and confused about the entire venture.

Why would this be? If you recall Core Focus #1 from the previous chapter, you'll know that one of the critical actions you must learn to do is generate targeted traffic.

Nothing happens until people click your affiliate links in order to have them directed to the solution you wish to offer them. Should they make a purchase, you get paid a commission for that sale. If not, you get nothing.

But getting people to take that first step, before you can earn a commission, requires an investment on your part: time and money.

A cost of time in relation to traffic is commonly referred to as 'free traffic'; a cost of money in relation to traffic refers to 'paid advertising'.

As the saying goes, *"Time is money."* Therefore, there's always a cost in getting traffic, and every single person who clicks your affiliate link has been paid for by you in one form or another.

Value Your Time

Time is our most precious commodity; when a day is gone, it's gone forever. So how much time it takes to get even one commission matters.

This realization led me to value my time more than anything else. In terms of traffic, that meant turning my attention to paying for it with money via various forms of paid advertising rather than investing my time into so called 'free' methods.

But here's the catch: the cost of getting a person to click my link through paid advertising has been rising steadily for years. Whilst in the past that traffic would cost pennies per visitor, today my cost per click (CPC) is dollars per visitor.

This trend will likely continue because of supply and demand; when the demand for traffic by advertisers rises faster than the amount of traffic available, it drives the cost up.

I noticed this trend happening years ago and knew the days were numbered for the average person to start from scratch and make a profit in this game. The trend has continued and shows no sign of stopping. For this reason, traditional affiliate marketing as everyone knows it no longer works for the average person starting out.

In the good ol' days of affiliate marketing, you could easily multiply the money you spent on traffic into vast profits. Let me give an example: if you got prospects clicking your affiliate link at a cost of $0.10 per click and 100 people clicked your link, it would cost you $10. Out of the 100 people, you end up making two sales. If, let's say, your commission was $20 per sale, you got paid $40 in commissions. So, you spent $10 and made $40 back. That means you quadrupled your money. Traffic costs were low and profits were high from simple product sales.

Today, to get your advertising going and get people to click your affiliate link may cost $1, $2, $3 or more per click. If you get paid $20 for each sale you generate, and if you send the same 100 visitors to the offer and make the same number of sales, which was two, you still earn $40 in commissions. But to send the 100 visitors to the website you paid a total of $200! That means you spent $200 and made back $40, losing $160.

That is the reality of what we face today. The cost of online advertising has risen to where it's no longer profitable for the average person starting out in the affiliate marketing business.

Now, you may be shouting, *"But, Dean. I see*

people screaming about making massive money as an affiliate online all the time." And you'd be right. There ARE people making massive incomes as an affiliate online. But here's a secret: most of them have built a customer base by selling their own products, and it's easy to promote affiliate offers and make money when you have customers to recommend them to. What I'm talking about is the end of traditional affiliate marketing for the little guy, the man or woman who's starting out from scratch wanting to build a business promoting other businesses' products and services.

Years ago, when my profit margins got smaller and smaller due to the rising cost of advertising, I knew I had to do something about it before it was too late. To combat the problem, I developed a powerful and highly effective sales system that not only brought our profits back, but far exceeded where they had ever historically been. The rest of the book is devoted to teaching you our secret.

CHAPTER 7
THE PERFECT PATH TO
7 FIGURES

Surfing the web for the seemingly countless different ways to build a business on the Internet can be overwhelming and confusing. I'm going to simplify it for you through a three-phase plan I've devised.

I didn't just pluck this plan from thin air; it's the exact path that I followed to escape a day job I hated, to build my own profitable business from home as my own boss selling millions worth of products online.

During the years since, I've perfected this plan and created the three core programs we offer in my company, each specifically built to take you from the ground up, starting from scratch to growing a profitable online business and scaling it to a 7-figure level.

Let's now look at the three phases of this plan.

Phase One: The Connector

In this first phase, you will leverage other businesses' product(s) and receive a commission on sales you generate as an affiliate marketer. You will gain the knowledge and understanding of exactly how this business model works in the current economy so that you can make sales profitably.

You will learn the fundamentals of Internet marketing and develop the skills you need to be able to reach a certain group of people online and get your messages in front of them. Connecting a group of people with products or services that solve their problems is what will generate income for you.

Primarily, you will need to learn the first three of the four core areas of focus: generating traffic, capturing potential prospects onto your email list, and following up with them effectively to refer them to the products and solutions you are promoting. You will not be the one doing the fourth core area of focus: building and managing the sales system.

This was how I was able to leave my day job and how you can too! However, as you now know, traditional affiliate marketing no longer works like it used to and it's only going to worsen. You need the next generation of affiliate marketing, which I shall soon share.

You can take your results in this phase as far and high as you so wish. I know affiliates that make millions per year, so it's possible to get everything you want in this phase if you want to, although some people progress no further.

On average, though, I like to set a guideline income of anywhere between $3,000 and $10,000 per month in this phase, before moving onto the next.

Phase Two: The Creator

In this second phase, you will sell your own products and/or services online. At this point in your business, you will have learned and developed key skills that got you to a certain level of income. Taking that knowledge, you can start to learn additional skills to achieve higher levels of success in multiple different ways.

In phase two, you're taking control of the fourth core area of focus for yourself: the sales system. In doing so, you get to make more of an impact on the lives of others because you can now harness your knowledge and the valuable experience you have gained to create and offer your own products or services.

With your own products, you will be acquiring your own customers and providing the solution to their problems directly yourself. In contrast, in phase one another company was providing the solution, and you acted as the bridge that connected the customer to them.

In phase two, your income is uncapped. You can take it to millions, tens of millions or more. However, there's a lot to learn at that stage and a lot of new skills that have to be acquired. For that reason, I recommend most start in phase one by leveraging other people's products and services to help get the skills you need to better succeed in phase two.

Phase Three: The Commander

This final phase is about taking areas of business and life to the next level. Its main purpose is to focus on systems and scale, essentially structuring your business to operate effectively without you needing to be there. In other words, the goal is to have a business operating 24/7 and running profitably with or without your presence.

Additionally, phase three will ensure that everything you have done to get here and what you will do going forward is making your dream life a lifelong reality. This phase will involve systems, others working for you and having affiliates promoting your products for you for commissions.

Although not a necessity, I recommend you are earning at least $100,000 per year in your business before moving to this phase.

There you have it, the perfect path to 7 figures. I've witnessed a lot in my online career, and one thing I can say for sure is that when people try and build a business outside of this three phase sequence, they struggle or take far longer than necessary to get anywhere.

Building a business requires learning many new skills. I believe the best way forward is to always take the path of least resistance to enable you to get results in the fastest way possible.

Let's now look beneath the surface of a modern-day profitable online business sales system that combats the rising cost of online advertising and allows you to generate sales profitably.

CHAPTER 8

THE ICEBERG EFFECT

When I was a teenager, my mum took me to see the movie *Titanic*. Whilst the vision of the damage done by the collision was devastating, what stuck in my mind was what was happening beneath the surface, out of sight.

Most of us tend only to see the tip of the iceberg, unaware of what lies beneath the surface. This short-sightedness relates very much to how people do business, myself included when I first started out.

For instance, I believed that the products shown online were all the products available for purchase from any given business. The first time I got a hint that something else may be at play was when, a few days after buying a training course about online advertising for just under $100, I got a phone call from a sales rep. After asking how I was getting on with the training, the caller asked if I would like more direct, hands-on help in starting my online business.

For the next thirty minutes or so, I chatted with the caller, answering several questions and providing details of why I wanted to have an online business. Soon enough they told me I had qualified to speak with a second person, who had the authority to accept me into their coaching program. A time and date for the call was scheduled and we parted ways.

During that second call, I learned more about the offer, and that the cost to join was $6,000 for the six-week program. After much consideration, I decided the program wasn't something I wanted.

Let us analyse, though, what had happened. I had made a purchase online for a low-priced product and soon after was being offered a much more valuable product at a premium price, which, though I declined on that day, others likely bought.

After giving this experience some thought, I wondered how many people, daily, purchased that $6,000 program. The potential of the numbers involved was mind blowing, and I began to run through different scenarios in my head. *"Just one sale per day would be over $2.1 million in a year. Imagine if they are making 2 sales a day, 3, 4, 5 or even more a day?!"* I thought to myself.

For the first time in my online venture, I began to understand two principles that have today played a huge role in the success of my company. First, just like an iceberg, what you see on the surface isn't the complete picture of everything that's going on in a business. Second, the higher the price of a product, the larger the profit can be, and therefore the faster you can reach your dream life income.

Whilst I didn't know what to do with this information at that time, years later it would change everything for me and those with whom I work.

YOU DON'T KNOW WHAT YOU DON'T KNOW

In the early years of my Internet venture trying to figure out affiliate marketing, I believed you got paid commissions on all sales made to the customers you referred to a business.

As it turns out, that isn't how traditional affiliate marketing works. You get paid on certain sales and not on others, or as I now say, you only benefit from the tip of the iceberg. In other words, as a typical affiliate marketer you make commissions from the select lower-priced product sales visible above the surface, but not for any future sales that take place beneath the surface.

The thing is, it's those sales that take place beneath the surface that tend to produce all the profit, like in the example of that $6,000 program I was offered after I'd purchased the $100 product days earlier. With the traditional affiliate marketing model, you'd be paid a commission on making that initial $100 sale but nothing on the later $6,000 sale, even though it was your referred customer! In simple terms, you're cut out of the big bucks and miss out on the profit.

Today though, with the rising cost of advertising, those lower-priced product sales are, by and large, obsolete; they may at very best cover the cost of the advertising. To produce profit you must tap into what's beneath the surface.

To better grasp why this is the only way to remain profitable, you must understand that there are only three ways to grow any business.

THE ONLY THREE WAYS TO GROW ANY BUSINESS

Before I had the good fortune of getting access to a training video created by entrepreneur Jay Abraham, I had the belief that there are likely dozens of ways to grow a business. In fact there are just three, and understanding these helps make it even clearer why traditional affiliate marketing is dead for most people starting out.

1. Acquire More Customers

This may be obvious, but if a business has no customers then it's not going to remain in business. The more customers a business can acquire, the more sales it can make.

2. Sell More Products to New Customers at the Point of Sale

You'll find most businesses you encounter, both online and offline, to incorporate this strategy into their sales process. Think about the mega successful McDonald's chain, with their famous question, *"Would you like fries with that?"*

Simply offering an additional item at the point of sale multiplied the average revenue generated per customer.

Another example is exposing customers to other products at the same time you're selling them one. For instance, as you go through the checkout lane in the supermarket, loads of items, like gum, candy and magazines are at your fingertips for you to grab and add to your basket.

In another example, think about what happens in a restaurant, when the server takes your order and asks if you'd like to add a side order, such as vegetables or fries. Go into your local coffee shop and when you order a drink they'll likely ask if you'd like a shot of flavour in your drink, such as a vanilla shot, for an extra fee. They may also ask if you'd like to include a muffin or cookie with your order.

When you buy a digital product online, you may get presented with one or more offers to add an additional complementary product to your order, often at a special discounted price.

All of these are examples of businesses selling more to you at the point of sale, both to increase the value the customer receives, and to increase the value of the customer to the business.

You'll notice in each example the offers for additional items are optional. This is critically important. When you sell more to customers at the point of sale, it cannot be forced or you will detract value from the initial purchase and possibly sacrifice the potential for future business with that customer.

But if done correctly, these extra offerings are what will bring your business significant returns.

3. Get Your Customers to Buy from You More Often

Remember the story I shared about how after buying a product I received a call offering me additional coaching for a premium price? The company's aim was to bring me back to make an additional purchase at a point in future.

This is the third and final way to grow a business: to generate repeat sales by bringing your customers back to make additional purchases. When done correctly, this is the easiest and most profitable way to make sales, as at this point you have already paid the cost to acquire that customer, so any additional sales increase your returns.

The likelihood of repeat business rests, of course, on your customers getting value and receiving a positive experience from their previous purchase(s).

So, bottom line: get more customers, sell more products to new customers at the point of sale, and get customers to buy from you more often.

Of course, you're now wondering how to accomplish all three effectively and, more important, profitably. The answer: you need to look at the big picture.

THE BIG PICTURE

In my iceberg analogy there are two areas I focus on: what you see above the surface and what you don't see, beneath the surface. In comparison to an online-based business, there are also two main areas: the 'frontend' of the business and the 'backend' of the business. Let's look at both and how they tie into what you've learned so far about the three ways to grow any business.

The Frontend

The frontend of a business is the tip of the iceberg – the entry-level products and offers on clear view above the surface. It is where you capture people onto your email list to follow up with, acquire customers and aim to make additional sales at the point of sale.

It's the sales that occur in the frontend of a business on which product owners are typically willing to pay commissions to affiliates. However, these frontend sales may or may not be profitable. This is because the cost to acquire customers takes place in the frontend, and as you now know, these lower-priced offers alone may not be enough to recover the advertising costs.

The Backend

Using my iceberg analogy, the backend of a business is what takes place beneath the surface, out of sight. It's what a business offers to its customers after the initial acquisition process has taken place in the frontend, and where you make the bulk of your profit by offering further products and services to existing customers you've already paid the cost to acquire.

For instance, you are now reading my book, a product you paid a small sum to receive. This purchase allows me to acquire new customers like you into the frontend part of my business and sales process.

At the same time, if you ordered this book directly from my website, you were presented with two or three additional offers, special deals made available to you as a new customer at the point of sale. This still took place in the frontend of my business and sales process.

If you said 'yes' to any optional extras, you will have received even more value from us in the form of additional training, whilst at the same time spending more money with my company. Beyond this point is the backend of the business, as you are now a customer of mine with the potential for future business with my company if you want more of what we have to offer.

In summary, the frontend of a business is used to acquire new customers and increase the value of a customer at the point of sale. The backend of a business is used to add further value to a business's customers by providing them with additional solutions that can serve them whilst generating maximum profits and, as I've been touting all along, where you start to make big bucks.

As you now know, with traditional affiliate marketing you are typically not compensated for any sales in the backend of a business even though you generated the customer for them. As I have discussed earlier in this book, this factor, combined with the rising cost of getting traffic, is killing the chances of success for most people starting out.

Fear not though, there is a solution that you will soon discover.

First, let's put the frontend and the backend of my business model underneath a microscope to show the different types of sales and income streams contained within a highly profitable online business.

CHAPTER 9

MULTIPLE STREAMS
OF INCOME

When I was last employed, many years ago, I was paid a set amount of money on the same date towards the end of every month. I knew when I was getting it and how much I would receive.

Most people are the same; they typically have one regular source of income, whether it's a day job salary, pension or even state benefits. Having that predictable, regular income stream allows us to get by, pay bills, run a vehicle, keep a roof over our heads and put food on the table. In other words, that dependable source of income gives each of us some level of stability and security to plan and budget for what we can and cannot afford to do in our lives.

I will assume that you would not be reading this book right now if you were entirely happy with the level of your current income and/or the way in which you are earning it, and that's great because in getting this book you have made a commitment to do something about it.

However, one thing I will say is that having a regular income that has a degree of predictability and certainty is the best form of income there is, and for that reason I make it a huge focus in my online ventures and would encourage you to do the same.

Before we get too far ahead of ourselves here, I do want to be clear on something, because I'm the absolute opposite of the many so-called experts online that will feed you a line about being able to make untold fortunes with three clicks of your mouse!

Starting your own business naturally comes with risk and can lack certainty, financial or otherwise, until you establish certain things. But you should know, if you operate in the way that I will continue to explain throughout this book, you are setting yourself up for success in the best possible way.

Better yet, unlike your traditional day job or pension payments, with an online business you can have multiple streams of income that reward you in several different forms.

No longer do you have to accept one stream of income as the normal. With marketing and sales processes, you can offer a wide array of products and services that compensate you in different ways; let's now look at what they are.

THE TWO TYPES OF SALES

In your online business, two main types of sales provide income: one-time sales and recurring sales. These can be found in both the frontend and the backend of a business.

One Time Sales

One-time sales are just that: single, one-time purchases made for an item. An example would be buying a sandwich from a local store that you may or may not purchase from again in future.

Some one-time sales are small and provide little to no profit. But some are substantial, and even though you may collect only a single payment from the customer, they can provide significant profit margins (hint: the backend!).

Let's take this book as an example. Whilst it's a low-priced item that alone has no profit for the business, we also offer a range of solutions that you may want to pursue after reading it that sell anywhere from $1,000 up to many tens of thousands.

We call these high-value sales 'high-ticket products' or 'premium products'. These high-value solutions are typically what will generate significant profits for a business whilst also being the very best value for the customer.

Once, while teaching this concept at a small live event in the USA, I noticed a guy in the front row whose facial expression yelled, *"BS!"*

To help him over this self-limiting belief, we had a conversation that went something like this:

DEAN: *"Do you disagree with what I just shared?"*

JIM: *"Kind of. I just don't believe anyone would pay that kind of money."*

DEAN: *"Great, I'm glad you told me so I can help you. Am I correct your accent is from the UK?"*

JIM: *"Yes, I live just outside of London."*

DEAN: *"OK, out of interest how did you get to the USA?"*

JIM: *"I flew, why?"*

DEAN: *"What class did you fly?"*

JIM: *"Economy."*

DEAN: *"As you boarded the plane, did you notice you passed through business class seating?"*

JIM: *"Yeah."*

DEAN: *"Was the business class seating and setup better than that in economy?"*

JIM: *"Ha-ha. Yes, of course."*

DEAN: *"Do you think those seated in business had a better experience than you?"*

JIM: *"I guess so, yes."*

DEAN: *"Well, just so you know I flew here in the business section. I got to lie down in a fully reclining bed and had a great sleep for several hours. Whilst awake, I enjoyed two glasses of champagne, and for my meal I ate a delicious steak with vegetables and dauphinoise potatoes. What was your journey like?"*

JIM: *"HA-HA! Nothing like that. I sat next to this guy who kept elbowing me in his sleep, and we got served cold sandwiches for lunch."*

DEAN: *"OK, so you can see that even though we got to the same destination in the end, my journey to get here was by all accounts a better one. Would you agree?"*

JIM: *"100% I agree, but you paid way more than I did."*

DEAN: *"You're absolutely right. But out of interest, why didn't you pay for a better experience?"*

JIM: *"I would never pay those prices."*

DEAN: *"Well, my friend, that is why you think others also would not pay. But I can tell you this... On my flight over here, I didn't see a single empty seat in business. I'd say at least 50 others around me all enjoyed the premium experience of that flight. And let's not forget there was also a first class cabin where people paid 5 to 8 times more than I did for an even better experience than mine."*

From this conversation, you can summarize that some people will always want low cost or cheap, whilst others will always want the very best they can get. The latter will buy premium products from me and other ethical businesses, knowing that getting the very best experience and solution will ultimately yield the very best results in the fastest time possible and is therefore an investment for which it is worth paying.

For a premium price, they will let us mentor them to help them go to a higher level, without having to waste time going through relentless trial and error to find the answers.

In this way, they don't waste time going down the wrong path. And time, after all, is money. As my good friend James P. Friel once told me, *"You can climb a ladder but if it's leaning against the wrong building, what good is it?"* In other words, if you're taking action on the wrong things, you'll never get the desired outcome. You need the correct information and to take the correct actions in the correct sequence if you are to stand any chance of success today.

For that reason, I will constantly seek out coaching in all areas of my life and business when I want to improve in that area. Sure, you could spend the time to try and figure it out on your own, but why bother? Why put yourself through that when there are others that have already done it? To me, that makes no sense. Time is precious, after all.

Recurring Sales

Recurring sales are subscription-based payments that customers make on an ongoing basis until they decide to cancel. They offer a business stability and security and should be the backbone of your operation in some form or another.

To understand recurring sales, think about a gym membership or a magazine to which you're subscribed. In both examples, you're paying a monthly fee and, in exchange, receiving access to a product or service you can cancel any time. While I use both one-time sales and recurring sales, the latter is what has enabled me to buy an amazing home for my family, enjoy nice cars, take vacations, buy fun experiences, make investments, and to know with certainty all bills are covered.

Picture this scenario: let's imagine your current monthly outgoings, to cover all bills and essential payments, come to $1,500 per month. In your online business you have been promoting a membership-style offer that pays you $30 per month for each customer that signs up. Over a period of time, you refer 50 customers to the membership and are receiving $1,500 in monthly recurring commissions.

Your monthly bills and essential payments are now all covered with your recurring income! Can you imagine how much more comfortable you'd feel, knowing that any and every other income you make is extra on top? Now imagine that grows, 100 customers, 200 customer and more! That's the power of recurring income and why it's an integral part of any smart online entrepreneur's business.

ACHIEVING BOTH ONE TIME AND RECURRING INCOME

Now that you understand the concept of multiple streams of income via one-time income and recurring income, let's explore the inner workings of a highly profitable sales process.

First, before I break down the entire system for you, I want to share in the next chapter how I discovered a key part of the process that contributes towards its success.

CHAPTER 10
THE MOST POWERFUL WORD IN MARKETING

I am passionate about food. One of my favourite places to explore food is *Borough Market* in London, one of the largest and oldest food markets in the country, which has been serving people for over 1,000 years.

The first time I visited the market, I felt like a kid in a candy store. As you walk around, sensations and smells from foods from around the globe hit you, enticing the senses. That first day, I witnessed something that would eventually change my business forever.

I stood in the middle of a walkway in the cheese vendor section with vendors on either side, offering their products. On one side, a guy stood, hands on hips, offering a massive variety of cheeses for sale, but not a single customer looked at his products. On the other side, another business offered a similar variety of cheeses. But this stall had a long line of people queuing up and down the street to access it.

As I walked closer to investigate what the big attraction was, I noticed two guys working at the cheese stand dressed in clean white chef jackets. One had a large wooden board in his hands with six different types of cheese all chopped up into small cubes. Whenever the next person in line stepped forward, he'd hold out the board and invite them to try a different sample of each cheese for free, which many did.

Each time someone tried some free pieces, he'd ask them what their favourite was, and upon hearing their reply, ask if they wanted some to take home with them. Some said, 'No, thanks," and walked off. But many wanted to buy some cheese to take home, and the second guy took over to collect payment.

You may not think anything too special of what I've just described, as chances are you've experienced it many times yourself and understand how it works. But for the avoidance of doubt, let's be clear – the big attraction was the promise of 'try the cheese for free', the key word being 'FREE'. Such a simple concept and yet so genius. Who doesn't want something for *free*?

Fascinated with what I'd seen, during the days and weeks that followed, my mind was going full force to figure out how to apply this to my online business.

First, I investigated businesses and brands using this approach and how well it worked for them. It took little time to realize it was both common and highly effective.

For instance, I noticed the gym I attended offered a free one-month membership so you could try out the facilities before deciding whether to sign up. I saw a well-known coffee shop offering a free muffin with every large coffee to attract more people through the door. At the grocery store, I was offered a small free sample of a new milkshake being launched, and then asked if I would like to purchase a bottle.

Still, I couldn't figure out how this could translate to an online business like mine where we sold digital products. Sure, you can offer free digital downloads, and many people do, but what I was trying to figure out here was to do what I saw that day at Borough Market, to get customers pulling out their wallets to purchase using the power of 'free'.

Then, one day in 2015, something on the Internet caught my attention – a square graphic banner ad on a website I was visiting with a headline that read, *"FREE BOOK CLICK HERE."* I clicked the image and was immediately taken to Russell Brunson's website; he was an online entrepreneur I'd respected for many years. He wasn't offering a digital download of the book, but rather he was offering the physical copy for free! To receive the book in the mail, you only had to pay a small shipping and handling charge.

Russell had figured out what I had failed to do: he had turned a product of his into a physical item, a book, and was giving it away for free. Clearly Russell had calculated that he could afford to give away the book knowing some people who read it would want to buy more of his other products and services in the backend of his business.

I now was faced with two options: try and learn how it's done on my own or get Russell to teach it to me. The old me that used to struggle to get any results would have opted for the first option. But the wiser, smarter me knew there was only one path to walk, and so I reached out to Russell via Facebook and initiated a conversation.

After a few messages had been exchanged back and forth, Russell arranged for me to have a call with someone on his team. I did and found out I could get access to Russell and his knowledge if I invested a significant five-figure sum to join his mastermind program. I knew this was the turning point for me and so I made that investment, and within the months that followed, I'd go on to learn exactly how the 'free plus shipping' offer was done.

We finally had a unique and proven way to attract floods of perfect customers into my business leveraging the most powerful word in marketing: *free*. We could then proceed to offer more of our products to these customers, generating purchases for our recurring subscription products and premium programs, which, as mentioned earlier, currently range up to tens of thousands of dollars.

Now all we needed to do was to show the right people our free physical products and watch them take them, only paying a small shipping and handling charge.

With this understanding on how to get customers into the business, the next questions on your mind may be, "How do you make those additional sales at the time of purchase effectively?" and "How do you bring as many of those customers back to make purchases of our premium products?"

Answering those questions led to the highly successful sales model we employ today, suitably called *'The Ultimate Funnel'*.

CHAPTER 11
THE ULTIMATE FUNNEL

I was sitting in a bar at Seattle-Tacoma International Airport awaiting my flight to Boise, Idaho, where I'd be spending several days at a mastermind with some amazing entrepreneurs. As I sipped an ice-cold beer whilst watching a sports channel on the TV, my phone beeped. I grabbed it from my pocket to see a notification on the screen, telling me Russell Brunson was messaging me via Voxer.

Surprised and curious, I raced to open it. Never in my wildest imagination could I have predicted what was about to happen.

"Hey, Dean, it's Russell. Hope you're ok, man. Listen, I wondered if you'd come and talk on stage at our event Funnel Hacking Live and share your business model with my tribe?"

I rushed to respond and confirm how exciting that

would be and what an honour it was to be asked. Once the event plans began to form, I glanced at the ticket sales website. As I scrolled down the page, I saw my picture with the headline: *'The Ultimate Funnel'*. I couldn't believe it.

The guy that had popularized the sales funnel process had stated, for all to see, that I had developed the ULTIMATE sales funnel. What an overwhelming sense of achievement. I couldn't wait to share it with my wife and mum.

I've given talks over the years at many events but

nothing like this. This event was expected to have over 3,000 attendees, and the feeling of getting up on that stage was incredible, albeit daunting. Ten years earlier, I had been at the lowest point in my life on the brink of bankruptcy. And here I was taking to the stage in front of thousands of entrepreneurs. Unbelievable!

WHAT IS THE ULTIMATE FUNNEL?

The Ultimate Funnel is a superior, more profitable kind of sales funnel. If you're unfamiliar with a sales funnel, let me first explain what that means: a sales funnel refers to the sales process that you send prospects and customers through to introduce them to yourself, your business and your offers. It comprises multiple stages, each with its own specific desired outcome, which work together to turn website visitors into prospects, prospects into customers, and customers into repeat customers. Some of these stages occur in the frontend of the business, whilst others occur in the backend of the business.

There are many different types of sales funnels that can be used for a variety of purposes and specific desired outcomes. Whilst in 'Phase One' of your business using the 'Connector' model, you will not be creating the offers or building complete sales funnels yourself; it is, however, still important to understand the process in full to build your business profitably.

In my *Ultimate Funnel*, five stages work together to form a highly profitable Internet business system. This system leads prospects through a sequence of steps to give them value, turn them into customers, and keep bringing them back for more as they progress. Each stage has its own type of product, offer and purpose.

The stages are:

1. Lead Capture
2. Customer Acquisition
3. Value Maximization
4. Recurring Revenue
5. Premium Products

Let's look at each of these stages in detail now. You may notice how things begin to come together between the *Four Core Areas of Focus* discussed earlier in the book and the breakdown of the *Ultimate Funnel*.

STAGE ONE: LEAD CAPTURE

The first stage of the *Ultimate Funnel* is to capture and build an email list of potential customers, or as we call them, 'leads'. If you recall back to earlier in the book, we achieve this by offering something of value in exchange for their contact information, usually their email address.

Whilst I don't want to bore you by repeating myself, it's important that you have a clear and complete understanding of each stage of the Ultimate Funnel, so allow me to reiterate for clarity's sake.

To capture potential customers' email addresses, we offer some form of content, either video, text, graphic or even software. This could be a digital PDF report on a subject matter, video training or tutorial for something, or even a case study about a result that has been achieved.

What's important are two things: what you're offering attracts the ideal type of person for the products you wish to promote; and the bribe you're offering for free is highly desirable to that person to have them want to opt in to receive it.

On the next page is an example of one of our lead capture pages.

100% FREE VIDEO

Learn How I Went From Working 9 Hours Per Day As A Construction Worker To Only a Few Hours Per Day From My Computer

If You Have A Computer, An Internet Connection, And A Desire For More In Life... You'll Want To See This Video

Send Me The Free Video

🔒 **Privacy Policy:** Your Information is 100% Secure

At this stage you are now capturing ideal prospects' email addresses and building your list. By following up with them we move people on to stage two of the *Ultimate Funnel*.

STAGE TWO: CUSTOMER ACQUISITION

In stage two, we focus on converting as many of our leads into paying customers as possible. We do this by presenting them with an initial frontend offer. This is a low-priced product and therefore a low-risk purchase that they will make quickly, with little decision required.

Prior to learning from Russell Brunson how to do the 'physical product free plus shipping' style offer, I'd sell digital products priced between $5 and $20, and we'd typically get between 1% and 2% of our leads buying and becoming customers.

After we switched to the 'free plus shipping' style offers, the 1 – 2% uptake increased all the way up to a 5% uptake, and even as high as 15% in some cases. That means without any increase in traffic, switching to the offer of a 'free plus shipping' style frontend product has allowed us to multiply the number of customers we're getting without any extra spend on advertising!

The reason I believe this to be the case is that a physical item that people can actually hold in their hands has a higher perceived level of value in comparison to intangible digital products. Combine that with the fact they can get the item for free makes it a big win for them! And we're still getting a customer because they are still making a transaction with us to pay for the shipping and handling costs.

On the next page is an example of one of our customer acquisition offers.

At this point in the process, we are now converting the prospects captured in stage one into customers, and it's time to have the *Ultimate Funnel* sell more to these customers at the point of sale.

STAGE THREE: VALUE MAXIMIZATION

McDonald's created arguably the most famous phrase in value maximization history with their simple question: *"Want fries with that?"*

Their goal was to get a customer who ordered a burger to purchase multiple items and spend more money, a strategy widely adopted by many businesses today.

In stage three of the *Ultimate Funnel*, value maximization, our goal is just that, to make additional sales to our new customers at the point of sale. We are maximizing value for the customer by giving him/her the chance to get more of what they want and/or need from us and maximizing the value for the business by increasing the amount the customer spends with us at the point of sale. These types of offers are referred to as either upsells, or, if they will never again be available, one-time offers (OTO).

These offers will depend on the business and could either be more of what they just purchased on the frontend or complementary products that would benefit them.

For example, when someone orders a copy of this book from my website, I know they are interested in the topic of affiliate marketing, so for my upsell offers I would consider what other areas these customers would be interested in. It could be traffic generation or advertising, email list building or perhaps even copywriting.

Typically, the upsell offers will be priced higher than the initial frontend purchase but not so high that the customer would need to walk away and think about it. We want the customer to say '*yes*' there and then to the upsell offers.

By presenting these upsell offers in the final stage of the frontend of the business, our goal is to recoup most of, if not all, the advertising costs we spent to acquire the customer.

In doing so, anything they purchase from this point on adds to the profit and increases our return on investment, which happens in stages four and five of the *Ultimate Funnel.*

On the next page is an example of one of our value maximization offers.

STAGE FOUR: RECURRING REVENUE

In 2009, I attended a small marketing event in England hosted by Lee McIntyre. During the two days of that workshop, Lee shared his business model, what it was, how it worked, why it worked, and the results of it working. This showed me how they were making six figures a month largely from a membership site. I'd heard of the concept before but had no clue of its power or how to do it.

Early on in that workshop, Lee showed how they had over 1,000 people in a membership site of theirs, each paying $97 per month to be a member. It got my attention, that's for sure.

At the time, my income online came from selling one-time payment products. That meant that to maintain my level of income, or grow it, I had to continually find new customers.

Recurring income, otherwise known as continuity income, would solve that by ensuring, through membership subscription, that people paid monthly for a product until they decided to cancel.

This concept had great appeal, and soon after the workshop I looked for an opportunity to apply it and add recurring income to my business.

My first membership site happened almost by accident. After Alex's coaching program in 2008, I'd kept in touch with several other students in the program. One of them had a company in the US through which he'd help clients get traffic to their websites via a search engine optimization (SEO) strategy.

I asked him if he'd be interested in partnering with me on a project where we could take his knowledge of getting traffic and package it into a membership site using what I had learned.

We both loved the idea and so it began. During the weeks that followed, we created a membership site that delivered monthly training to teach his traffic generation system, and members could access the training for $97 per month. The project exploded bigger and faster than we could ever have predicted, so much so that within just four months we had our first six-figure month!

Unfortunately, we were inexperienced and made a lot of mistakes, and within a year the project was dead. My takeaway, though, was the power of recurring income for providing stability and security in life.

For that reason, I have implemented multiple membership style offers into my *Ultimate Funnel* system. We have memberships for ongoing access to software and memberships for ongoing access to training. As my customers flow through the process, they get presented with these offers at suitable times and every time someone joins, the recurring income grows.

On the next page is an example of one of our recurring revenue offers.

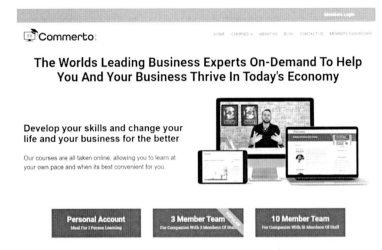

With that said, let's dive into the final stage of the *Ultimate Funnel,* which also delivers upon the same outcome of bringing our customers back to make additional purchases.

STAGE FIVE: PREMIUM PRODUCTS

In 2011 my phone rang. It was Alex, my first mentor. He asked me if I'd consider moving from England to Wales, where he was located, to work on some projects together.

Intrigued, I asked what he had in mind. He told me a mentor of his had shared with him something they were doing that had increased their income and profits like never before. I'm talking five and six-figure DAYS!

Alex told me a mentor of his was getting the customers of his lower-priced frontend products on the phone and in doing so offering them higher value solutions to their problems. In this example they were making sales of coaching programs on the phone that sold for many thousands of dollars. Immediately, I recalled the day I received the phone call after buying a lower-priced product and was subsequently offered the $6,000 coaching program. I knew people were doing this, and now I had the chance to learn how for myself!

I could hear the excitement in Alex's voice and knew this was a move I had to make. Within a matter of weeks, I had packed my bags, left England and moved to Wales, where Alex and I then began our plans. Soon enough, we had signed a lease on an office and planned out the coaching program we would offer.

Alex detailed the process of how this would work. We didn't want to cold call masses of people and try to convince them to listen to us. We wanted people coming to us who already wanted our help and were interested in what we had to offer. Alex taught me how this would be done, so we developed a strategy to engineer that.

We created a video presentation that went into the details of things and how we could help them grow a business online using our methods. At the end of the video, we invited the viewer to apply for a phone call with us to discuss the details of the program. We sent the video to our email lists and sure enough we started receiving applications to talk with us.

The day we started making our phone calls, we sat on the floor of our large open-plan office. There were no desks or chairs. All we had were two phones on the floor, two note pads and pens.

Though I was nervous about making the phone calls, as I had never done this type of sales before, all jitteriness disappeared once that first sale came, changing my mindset, and life, forever.

Trying my best to remain calm, I sent them a payment link and moments later hit refresh. There it was, a big juicy $1,000 payment in my PayPal account!

Filled with immense excitement, the two of us continued to dial all day long, and by the end of that afternoon we'd made ten sales and had $10,000 in the bank from just one day of selling on the phone.

That single day taught me two of the biggest lessons of my business career:

1. Making premium-priced product sales is the fastest way to make big money and reach your dream life.

2. Getting on the phone with people that are interested in those premium products is the best way to make premium product sales.

As time went on, we improved this strategy whilst also raising our premium product prices and later hired others to make the phone calls and sell for us through processes we developed.

Alex and I worked together for about six months before both heading in our own directions, armed with this full system of having other people selling premium-priced products for us all day every day. In the years since, we've used this strategy within our *Ultimate Funnels* to sell thousands of our premium solutions, ranging from $1,000 up to as much as $30,000.

Below is an example of one of our premium
product application pages.

So, there you have it, the five stages of the
Ultimate Funnel system, each working together
from beginning to end to deliver increasing
amounts of value to the people flowing through it,

whilst increasing the revenue and profit earned over time.

I've covered a lot and your head might be whirling to comprehend it all. To simplify the process, the following steps show you exactly how everything works when operated together as a well-oiled machine:

Step One

We send people to a simple capture page where they're offered something relevant and of value for free in exchange for their email address. Once they enter their email address, three things happen:

1. They're added to our email list
2. They begin receiving daily emails from us
3. We present details of our frontend offer

through access to coaching, mentors, mastermind communities, and often done-for-you solutions.

When our customers invest in themselves and into one or more of our premium programs, everyone wins. The customers receive the very best solutions we, as a company, can provide. In turn, we increase our profits in the backend, often to the tune of many thousands of dollars.

This allows us to provide everything they need to succeed. Additionally, we have the profit to reinvest into reaching more people, thus increasing the positive impact we as a company are making.

With a complete *Ultimate Funnel* at your disposal, which provides multiple streams of income throughout the entire sales process, from low-priced one-time sales, to recurring revenue and premium product sales, you then invest your time, effort and resources into the *Four Core Areas of Focus*. These are: driving traffic, capturing potential customers onto your email list, following up via email, and making offers of the frontend product within *Ultimate Funnels*.

In doing so, your goal is to generate the level of profit you require to live your dream life as calculated earlier in the book.

CONCLUSION AND FREE GIFT

My goal throughout this book was to shine a light on why I believe traditional affiliate marketing no longer works for the average person starting out, and how, through an *Ultimate Funnel* that compensates you on everything your referred customers purchase, in both the frontend and backend, you can profitably grow an Internet-based business.

In time, if you so wish, you can and should build your own *Ultimate Funnel*, filled with your own products and services on offer. Until you reach that phase of your journey, I recommend taking what you have learned throughout this book to seek out suitable affiliate opportunities that meet the criteria you now know to be essential to the profitability of your business.

This means seeking affiliate programs that not only compensate you for the lower-priced frontend product sales you generate, but additionally will pay you a commission on all future purchases made by the customers you refer to them, including recurring revenue purchases and premium product purchases.

Sadly, these type of affiliate programs are rare; most companies keep all the backend revenue for themselves, and that's just how traditional affiliate marketing sadly operates. They are out there, though, and now you are fully aware of what you need, you are equipped with the information and knowledge required to build a highly profitable Internet business as an affiliate marketer.

Never forget, success in business is not just about making sales; it's about making sales PROFITABLY.

When you are ready, you can take what I have shared throughout this book as a blueprint of what you need to focus on doing to grow your business.

To find out more about how my team and I work with you in this phase of your business, I have prepared a special bonus gift for you. I've produced an online masterclass version of this book that, as my thank you for being a reader, I'm giving for free.

Towards the end of the masterclass you will be able to find out more about our *Internet Profits Accelerator* program, designed specifically for those wanting to grow a profitable affiliate-based business on the Internet using *Ultimate Funnels*.

To access your free bonus masterclass and find out more about *Internet Profits Accelerator*, please visit

IcebergEffectBonus.com

Thank you for reading. Here's to your success and creating the dream life you desire.

Dean Holland

RESOURCES

Throughout this book I have mentioned tools I use. Please go to the following URL for a full list of tools I use or recommend.

IcebergEffect.com/resources